MY SHOWER
MOMENTS

JOURNAL

INTRODUCTION

Thanks for purchasing your very own copy of My Shower Moments journal. This journal is an extension of the book 'Shower Moments'. If you have this journal there is a high chance that you have read Shower Moments and have begun your journaling journey.

This book represents your personal journey to self-discovery and self-mastery. It is a space for you to connect and/or reconnect with yourself on a deep and personal level, writing down your IDEAs about life in general but more specifically, your life's path, dreams and goals. If you are inclined to do something in your life that helps you and others live a more fulfilled life, journalling is a good way to get clear about your IDEAs; your Inspirations, Dreams, Experiments, and Analyses. Use this space in whatever format you wish, whether it's free flowing or something more structured. The pages are only structured in so far as to provide you with a space to write the date, because dates are important.

They provide you with a timestamp for your IDEAs and you can look back and notice your journey and how far you've come.

You'll find quotes and/or words of encouragement and inspiration flowing through this journal. These small gems have been taken from the book 'Shower Moments' to serve you well as you go through your journaling process. I hope journaling is a productive exercise for you that propels you forward as you get closer to achieving your goals.

With much love,

Josephine Samson

"Not all storms come to disrupt your life,
some come to clear your path."

– Paolo Coelho

Date:__/__/____

Inspirations, Dreams, Experiments, Analyses

_____
_____
_____
_____
_____
_____
_____
_____
_____
_____
_____
_____
_____
_____
_____
_____
_____
_____
_____

Date:__/__/____

Inspirations, Dreams, Experiments, Analyses

_____

_____

_____

_____

_____

_____

_____

_____

_____

_____

_____

_____

_____

_____

_____

_____

_____

_____

Date:__/__/____

Inspirations, Dreams, Experiments, Analyses

_____

_____

_____

_____

_____

_____

_____

_____

_____

_____

_____

_____

_____

_____

_____

_____

_____

_____

_____

Just like the sun shines, life lifes.

IDEAs

Date:__/__/____

Inspirations, Dreams, Experiments, Analyses

_____

_____

_____

_____

_____

_____

_____

_____

_____

_____

_____

_____

_____

_____

_____

_____

_____

_____

_____

_____

Date:__/__/____

Inspirations, Dreams, Experiments, Analyses

_____

_____

_____

_____

_____

_____

_____

_____

_____

_____

_____

_____

_____

_____

_____

_____

_____

_____

_____

_____

Date:__/__/____

Inspirations, Dreams, Experiments, Analyses

_____
_____
_____
_____
_____
_____
_____
_____
_____
_____
_____
_____
_____
_____
_____
_____
_____
_____
_____
_____

All roads lead back to you.

Date:__/__/____

Inspirations, Dreams, Experiments, Analyses

_____
_____
_____
_____
_____
_____
_____
_____
_____
_____
_____
_____
_____
_____
_____
_____
_____
_____
_____

Date:__/__/____

Inspirations, Dreams, Experiments, Analyses

_____

_____

_____

_____

_____

_____

_____

_____

_____

_____

_____

_____

_____

_____

_____

_____

_____

_____

_____

_____

_____

IDEAs

Date:__/__/____

Inspirations, Dreams, Experiments, Analyses

_____

_____

_____

_____

_____

_____

_____

_____

_____

_____

_____

_____

_____

_____

_____

_____

_____

_____

_____

IDEAs

Other people's problem is not me.

Date:__/__/____

Inspirations, Dreams, Experiments, Analyses

_____

_____

_____

_____

_____

_____

_____

_____

_____

_____

_____

_____

_____

_____

_____

_____

_____

_____

_____

Date:__/__/____

Inspirations, Dreams, Experiments, Analyses

_____

_____

_____

_____

_____

_____

_____

_____

_____

_____

_____

_____

_____

_____

_____

_____

_____

_____

_____

Date:__/__/____

Inspirations, Dreams, Experiments, Analyses

_____

_____

_____

_____

_____

_____

_____

_____

_____

_____

_____

_____

_____

_____

_____

_____

_____

_____

_____

_____

_____

Mindset is everything:
if you think you can, you can;
if you think you can't, you can't.

IDEAs

Date:__/__/____

Inspirations, Dreams, Experiments, Analyses

_____
_____
_____
_____
_____
_____
_____
_____
_____
_____
_____
_____
_____
_____
_____
_____
_____
_____
_____

Date:__/__/____

Inspirations, Dreams, Experiments, Analyses

_____

_____

_____

_____

_____

_____

_____

_____

_____

_____

_____

_____

_____

_____

_____

_____

_____

_____

Date:__/__/____

Inspirations, Dreams, Experiments, Analyses

_____

_____

_____

_____

_____

_____

_____

_____

_____

_____

_____

_____

_____

_____

_____

_____

_____

_____

_____

IDEAs

Keep it moving with style and grace.

Date:__/__/____

Inspirations, Dreams, Experiments, Analyses

_____
_____
_____
_____
_____
_____
_____
_____
_____
_____
_____
_____
_____
_____
_____
_____
_____
_____
_____
_____

Date:__/__/____

Inspirations, Dreams, Experiments, Analyses

_____

_____

_____

_____

_____

_____

_____

_____

_____

_____

_____

_____

_____

_____

_____

_____

_____

_____

Date:__/ __/ ____

Inspirations, Dreams, Experiments, Analyses

_____

_____

_____

_____

_____

_____

_____

_____

_____

_____

_____

_____

_____

_____

_____

_____

_____

_____

_____

IDEAs

You have everything
you need right here, right now.

IDEAs

Date:__/__/____

Inspirations, Dreams, Experiments, Analyses

_____
_____
_____
_____
_____
_____
_____
_____
_____
_____
_____
_____
_____
_____
_____
_____
_____
_____
_____

Date:__/__/____

Inspirations, Dreams, Experiments, Analyses

_____

_____

_____

_____

_____

_____

_____

_____

_____

_____

_____

_____

_____

_____

_____

_____

_____

_____

_____

_____

IDEAs

Date:__/__/____

Inspirations, Dreams, Experiments, Analyses

_____

_____

_____

_____

_____

_____

_____

_____

_____

_____

_____

_____

_____

_____

_____

_____

_____

_____

_____

IDEAs

Own your shit!

Or your shit will own you!

IDEAs

Date:__/__/____

Inspirations, Dreams, Experiments, Analyses

_____

_____

_____

_____

_____

_____

_____

_____

_____

_____

_____

_____

_____

_____

_____

_____

_____

_____

_____

Date:__/__/____

Inspirations, Dreams, Experiments, Analyses

_____

_____

_____

_____

_____

_____

_____

_____

_____

_____

_____

_____

_____

_____

_____

_____

_____

_____

_____

Date:__/__/____

Inspirations, Dreams, Experiments, Analyses

_____
_____
_____
_____
_____
_____
_____
_____
_____
_____
_____
_____
_____
_____
_____
_____
_____
_____
_____
_____
_____

IDEAs

No matter how bad things get,
you have to find the strength to keep smiling.

IDEAs

Date:__/__/____

Inspirations, Dreams, Experiments, Analyses

_____
_____
_____
_____
_____
_____
_____
_____
_____
_____
_____
_____
_____
_____
_____
_____
_____
_____
_____
_____
_____

Date:__/__/____

Inspirations, Dreams, Experiments, Analyses

_____

_____

_____

_____

_____

_____

_____

_____

_____

_____

_____

_____

_____

_____

_____

_____

_____

_____

Date:__/__/____

Inspirations, Dreams, Experiments, Analyses

_____

_____

_____

_____

_____

_____

_____

_____

_____

_____

_____

_____

_____

_____

_____

_____

_____

_____

Everything has a purpose
and serves a function.

IDEAs

Date:__/__/____

Inspirations, Dreams, Experiments, Analyses

_____
_____
_____
_____
_____
_____
_____
_____
_____
_____
_____
_____
_____
_____
_____
_____
_____
_____
_____

Date:__/__/____

Inspirations, Dreams, Experiments, Analyses

_____

_____

_____

_____

_____

_____

_____

_____

_____

_____

_____

_____

_____

_____

_____

_____

_____

_____

_____

Date:__/__/____

Inspirations, Dreams, Experiments, Analyses

_____
_____
_____
_____
_____
_____
_____
_____
_____
_____
_____
_____
_____
_____
_____
_____
_____
_____
_____

IDEAs

Pay attention to the angels around you.

Date:__/__/____

Inspirations, Dreams, Experiments, Analyses

_____
_____
_____
_____
_____
_____
_____
_____
_____
_____
_____
_____
_____
_____
_____
_____
_____
_____
_____
_____

Date:__/__/____

Inspirations, Dreams, Experiments, Analyses

_____

_____

_____

_____

_____

_____

_____

_____

_____

_____

_____

_____

_____

_____

_____

_____

_____

_____

Date:___/ ___/ _____

Inspirations, Dreams, Experiments, Analyses

_____

_____

_____

_____

_____

_____

_____

_____

_____

_____

_____

_____

_____

_____

_____

_____

_____

_____

_____

_____

IDEAs

...the past only exists in our memories
and the future exists in our construction.

Date:__ / __ / ____

Inspirations, Dreams, Experiments, Analyses

_____

_____

_____

_____

_____

_____

_____

_____

_____

_____

_____

_____

_____

_____

_____

_____

_____

_____

_____

_____

Date:__/__/____

Inspirations, Dreams, Experiments, Analyses

_____

_____

_____

_____

_____

_____

_____

_____

_____

_____

_____

_____

_____

_____

_____

_____

_____

_____

_____

Date:__/__/____

Inspirations, Dreams, Experiments, Analyses

_____

_____

_____

_____

_____

_____

_____

_____

_____

_____

_____

_____

_____

_____

_____

_____

_____

_____

_____

IDEAs

When you take life to that granular level of now,
you begin to notice just how expansive things can be.

Date:__/__/____

Inspirations, Dreams, Experiments, Analyses

_____
_____
_____
_____
_____
_____
_____
_____
_____
_____
_____
_____
_____
_____
_____
_____
_____
_____
_____
_____

Date:__/__/____

Inspirations, Dreams, Experiments, Analyses

_____

_____

_____

_____

_____

_____

_____

_____

_____

_____

_____

_____

_____

_____

_____

_____

_____

_____

_____

Date:__/__/____

Inspirations, Dreams, Experiments, Analyses

_____

_____

_____

_____

_____

_____

_____

_____

_____

_____

_____

_____

_____

_____

_____

_____

_____

_____

_____

_____

Sometimes take a moment to pause, breathe,
and notice what you have in front of you.

Date:__/__/____

Inspirations, Dreams, Experiments, Analyses

_____

_____

_____

_____

_____

_____

_____

_____

_____

_____

_____

_____

_____

_____

_____

_____

_____

_____

_____

Date:__/__/____

Inspirations, Dreams, Experiments, Analyses

_____

_____

_____

_____

_____

_____

_____

_____

_____

_____

_____

_____

_____

_____

_____

_____

_____

_____

_____

Date:__/__/____

Inspirations, Dreams, Experiments, Analyses

_____
_____
_____
_____
_____
_____
_____
_____
_____
_____
_____
_____
_____
_____
_____
_____
_____
_____
_____

IDEAs

Start where you are.

IDEAs

Date:__/__/____

Inspirations, Dreams, Experiments, Analyses

_____
_____
_____
_____
_____
_____
_____
_____
_____
_____
_____
_____
_____
_____
_____
_____
_____
_____
_____
_____

Date:__/__/____

Inspirations, Dreams, Experiments, Analyses

_____

_____

_____

_____

_____

_____

_____

_____

_____

_____

_____

_____

_____

_____

_____

_____

_____

_____

Date:__/__/____

Inspirations, Dreams, Experiments, Analyses

_____
_____
_____
_____
_____
_____
_____
_____
_____
_____
_____
_____
_____
_____
_____
_____
_____
_____
_____

IDEAS

Preparation is key.
Always be ready.

Date:__/__/____

Inspirations, Dreams, Experiments, Analyses

_____
_____
_____
_____
_____
_____
_____
_____
_____
_____
_____
_____
_____
_____
_____
_____
_____
_____
_____
_____

Date:__/__/____

Inspirations, Dreams, Experiments, Analyses

_____

_____

_____

_____

_____

_____

_____

_____

_____

_____

_____

_____

_____

_____

_____

_____

_____

_____

_____

Date:__/__/____

Inspirations, Dreams, Experiments, Analyses

_____

_____

_____

_____

_____

_____

_____

_____

_____

_____

_____

_____

_____

_____

_____

_____

_____

_____

_____

_____

IDEAs

Be humble and stay grounded.

Date:__/__/____

Inspirations, Dreams, Experiments, Analyses

_____

_____

_____

_____

_____

_____

_____

_____

_____

_____

_____

_____

_____

_____

_____

_____

_____

_____

_____

Date:__/__/____

Inspirations, Dreams, Experiments, Analyses

_____

_____

_____

_____

_____

_____

_____

_____

_____

_____

_____

_____

_____

_____

_____

_____

_____

_____

_____

IDEAs

Date:__/__/____

Inspirations, Dreams, Experiments, Analyses

_____
_____
_____
_____
_____
_____
_____
_____
_____
_____
_____
_____
_____
_____
_____
_____
_____
_____
_____

IDEAS

Shine your light.

Date:__/__/____

Inspirations, Dreams, Experiments, Analyses

_____

_____

_____

_____

_____

_____

_____

_____

_____

_____

_____

_____

_____

_____

_____

_____

_____

_____

_____

Date:__/__/____

Inspirations, Dreams, Experiments, Analyses

_____

_____

_____

_____

_____

_____

_____

_____

_____

_____

_____

_____

_____

_____

_____

_____

_____

_____

Date:__/__/____

Inspirations: Dreams, Experiments, Analyses

_____

_____

_____

_____

_____

_____

_____

_____

_____

_____

_____

_____

_____

_____

_____

_____

_____

_____

_____

Love your mind.
Mend your heart.
Reach through your soul.

Date:__/__/____

Inspirations, Dreams, Experiments, Analyses

_____
_____
_____
_____
_____
_____
_____
_____
_____
_____
_____
_____
_____
_____
_____
_____
_____
_____
_____

Date:__/__/____

Inspirations, Dreams, Experiments, Analyses

_____

_____

_____

_____

_____

_____

_____

_____

_____

_____

_____

_____

_____

_____

_____

_____

_____

_____

IDEAs

Date:__/__/____

Inspirations, Dreams, Experiments, Analyses

Blank template page

I am a woman of value.

I bring value wherever I go.

Date:__/__/____

Inspirations, Dreams, Experiments, Analyses

_____
_____
_____
_____
_____
_____
_____
_____
_____
_____
_____
_____
_____
_____
_____
_____
_____
_____
_____
_____

Date:__/__/____

Inspirations, Dreams, Experiments, Analyses

_____
_____
_____
_____
_____
_____
_____
_____
_____
_____
_____
_____
_____
_____
_____
_____
_____
_____
_____

Date:__/__/____

Inspirations, Dreams, Experiments, Analyses

_____

_____

_____

_____

_____

_____

_____

_____

_____

_____

_____

_____

_____

_____

_____

_____

_____

_____

_____

_____

_____

IDEAs

I am a woman of worth.

I am worthy…

Date:__/__/____

Inspirations, Dreams, Experiments, Analyses

_____

_____

_____

_____

_____

_____

_____

_____

_____

_____

_____

_____

_____

_____

_____

_____

_____

_____

_____

Date:___/___/____

Inspirations, Dreams, Experiments, Analyses

_____

_____

_____

_____

_____

_____

_____

_____

_____

_____

_____

_____

_____

_____

_____

_____

_____

_____

_____

Date:__/__/____

Inspirations, Dreams, Experiments, Analyses

_____

_____

_____

_____

_____

_____

_____

_____

_____

_____

_____

_____

_____

_____

_____

_____

_____

_____

Be have and be life.

Date:__/__/____

Inspirations, Dreams, Experiments, Analyses

_____

_____

_____

_____

_____

_____

_____

_____

_____

_____

_____

_____

_____

_____

_____

_____

_____

_____

_____

Date:__/__/____

Inspirations, Dreams, Experiments, Analyses

_____

_____

_____

_____

_____

_____

_____

_____

_____

_____

_____

_____

_____

_____

_____

_____

_____

_____

_____

IDEAs

Date:__/__/____

Inspirations, Dreams, Experiments, Analyses

_____
_____
_____
_____
_____
_____
_____
_____
_____
_____
_____
_____
_____
_____
_____
_____
_____
_____
_____
_____

Moment by moment,
show up for yourself.

IDEAs

Date:__/__/____

Inspirations, Dreams, Experiments, Analyses

_____
_____
_____
_____
_____
_____
_____
_____
_____
_____
_____
_____
_____
_____
_____
_____
_____
_____
_____
_____

Date:__/__/____

Inspirations, Dreams, Experiments, Analyses

_____

_____

_____

_____

_____

_____

_____

_____

_____

_____

_____

_____

_____

_____

_____

_____

_____

_____

IDEAs

Date:__/__/____

Inspirations, Dreams, Experiments, Analyses

_____

_____

_____

_____

_____

_____

_____

_____

_____

_____

_____

_____

_____

_____

_____

_____

_____

_____

_____

_____

_____

IDEAs

Expect alignment,
because what's yours is already aligned.

Date:__/__/____

Inspirations, Dreams, Experiments, Analyses

_____
_____
_____
_____
_____
_____
_____
_____
_____
_____
_____
_____
_____
_____
_____
_____
_____
_____
_____
_____

Date:__/__/____

Inspirations, Dreams, Experiments, Analyses

_____

_____

_____

_____

_____

_____

_____

_____

_____

_____

_____

_____

_____

_____

_____

_____

_____

_____

_____

_____

IDEAs

Date:__/__/____

Inspirations, Dreams, Experiments, Analyses

_____
_____
_____
_____
_____
_____
_____
_____
_____
_____
_____
_____
_____
_____
_____
_____
_____
_____
_____
_____

IDEAs

With God, it's easy.

IDEAs

Date:__/__/____

Inspirations, Dreams, Experiments, Analyses

_____
_____
_____
_____
_____
_____
_____
_____
_____
_____
_____
_____
_____
_____
_____
_____
_____
_____
_____

Date:__/ __/ ____

Inspirations, Dreams, Experiments, Analyses

_____

_____

_____

_____

_____

_____

_____

_____

_____

_____

_____

_____

_____

_____

_____

_____

_____

_____

_____

IDEAs

Date:__/__/____

Inspirations, Dreams, Experiments, Analyses

_____

_____

_____

_____

_____

_____

_____

_____

_____

_____

_____

_____

_____

_____

_____

_____

_____

_____

_____

_____

IDEAs

What is that one thing
God gave you and told you to bring to the world?

Date:__/__/____

Inspirations, Dreams, Experiments, Analyses

_____
_____
_____
_____
_____
_____
_____
_____
_____
_____
_____
_____
_____
_____
_____
_____
_____
_____
_____
_____

Date:__/__/____

Inspirations, Dreams, Experiments, Analyses

_____

_____

_____

_____

_____

_____

_____

_____

_____

_____

_____

_____

_____

_____

_____

_____

_____

_____

_____

Date:__/__/____

Inspirations, Dreams, Experiments, Analyses

IDEAs

Keep moving,
no matter how small a step you take,
no matter how huge the obstacle,
no matter how loud the naysayers shout.

Date:__/__/____

Inspirations, Dreams, Experiments, Analyses

_____
_____
_____
_____
_____
_____
_____
_____
_____
_____
_____
_____
_____
_____
_____
_____
_____
_____
_____
_____

Date:__/__/____

Inspirations, Dreams, Experiments, Analyses

_____

_____

_____

_____

_____

_____

_____

_____

_____

_____

_____

_____

_____

_____

_____

_____

_____

_____

_____

IDEAs

Date:__/__/____

Inspirations, Dreams, Experiments, Analyses

_____
_____
_____
_____
_____
_____
_____
_____
_____
_____
_____
_____
_____
_____
_____
_____
_____
_____

9 781068 688928